ISLAND KITCHEN

AN ODE TO NEWFOUNDLAND

....

CHEF MARK MCCROWE

WITH SASHA OKSHEVSKY

 Canada Council **Conseil des Arts** for the Arts **du Canada**

Canada

 Newfoundland Labrador

We gratefully acknowledge the financial support of the Canada Council for the Arts, the Government of Canada through the Canada Book Fund (CBF), and the Government of Newfoundland and Labrador through the Department of Tourism, Culture and Recreation for our publishing program.

Printed on acid-free paper
Photography by Sasha Okshevsky and Mark McCrowe
Cover Design by Todd Manning
Layout by Joanne Snook-Hann and Todd Manning

Published by
CREATIVE PUBLISHERS
an imprint of CREATIVE BOOK PUBLISHING
a Transcontinental Inc. associated company
P.O. Box 8660, Stn. A
St. John's, Newfoundland and Labrador A1B 3T7

Printed in Canada

Library and Archives Canada Cataloguing in Publication

McCrowe, Mark, author
    Island kitchen : an ode to Newfoundland / Chef Mark McCrowe
with Sasha Okshevsky.

ISBN 978-1-77103-028-1 (pbk.)

    1. Cooking, Canadian--Newfoundland and Labrador style.
2. Cooking--Newfoundland and Labrador. 3. Cookbooks.
I. Okshevsky, Sasha, author II. Title.

TX715.6.M323 2014   641.59718   C2014-901357-4

ISLAND KITCHEN

AN ODE TO NEWFOUNDLAND

••••••••••••

CHEF MARK MCCROWE

WITH SASHA OKSHEVSKY

CREATIVE PUBLISHERS

St. John's, Newfoundland and Labrador
2014

BILL OF FARE

WELCOME | BIENVENUE

Island Kitchen is a cookbook and, like many others before it, it is a collection of recipes and photographs. However, this book is also a dedication, an ode to our province and its bounty. It represents the general feeling of pride and passion a person can have towards their home.

Newfoundland is beautiful, there's no question about it. From our shores to our outport communities, our cities and, God love them, our beautiful people. The culinary tradition in this province has developed over many years and has been influenced by people from all over the world. For centuries Newfoundland was an international fishing post. During this time, items were traded and recipes were passed down. The cold, unforgiving, lengthy winters combined with the long distances people had to travel resulted in the establishment of preservation techniques.

Newfoundland cuisine — well 'cuisine' may not be the right word to describe Newfoundland's food —is rustic and bold. It was primarily developed to fuel the hardworking fishermen who needed sustenance to get their work done. It's not a delicate, thoughtful cuisine but it is made with a lot of heart. There is a certain amount of satisfaction that comes from sharing a hot, tasty meal and something strong to drink with someone, especially when you don't have much more than each other.

These days food culture has taken off in so many ways, from cooking shows on TV, to food photos plastered all over social media, you can't escape it — food culture is taking over! It is exciting to see how people are becoming obsessed with cooking good food and, more importantly, staying away from unhealthy fast food as much as possible.

I'm a chef and have had a deep love for food for as long as I can remember. Growing up in Newfoundland is a very different experience than growing up in a large mainland city — though we still had all your classic Happy Meals and Spaghetti-O's. I spent a lot of time with my grandfather who was a fisherman, hunter and outdoorsman. Cod were gutted, salted and laid out on the flake to dry; rabbits were skinned and bottled for stews and moose were butchered and

treated in different ways to supply his family through the winter. We would fish for trout, salmon, squid, and scallops and hunt wild birds like turr and partridge. To see my nan take all these amazing natural ingredients and cook them up for us in a delicious meal really stuck with me.

After high school I moved to Vancouver and studied to be a chef at The Pacific Institute of Culinary Arts. It was definitely an eye-opener and further developed my love for food. I worked for some great chefs and learned how to treat food with respect and bring out its natural flavours. As a chef, if you are lucky enough, you can end up in a position where you have the freedom to create the dishes you want and present them on a menu. This is when you start to develop your own style. When I graduated I wanted to come home and cook for Newfoundlanders. I wanted to take what I'd learned and work on my version of Newfoundland food, which is a reflection of all the things I've seen throughout my life. It's an ingredient-driven cuisine, it is about taking a product from our island and not tampering with it, emphasizing its natural flavours without masking them.

Island Kitchen was born from many late night conversations with my friend and colleague Sasha Okshevsky, who has been a close friend of mine for years. We first met when I was a chef at AQUA in the early days before I took over the business. He was looking for some part-time work in the kitchen but he didn't have any experience in the restaurant industry. I hired him to help with appetizers, cleaning and whatever odd jobs we could find for him until he gained more knowledge of the industry. As time went on, I really got to know his character. We became good buddies and I could tell that he really had a passion for food and an interest in learning how to do things right. After years of working together we started talking about putting our ideas together in a cookbook. With Sasha's photography experience and my style of food, *Island Kitchen* quickly went from being a topic of conversation over drinks to a reality.

We want *Island Kitchen* to show you our vision of Newfoundland food. We want it to give you a feeling of pride or at least a curiosity about what we're cooking. It means the world to us and it involves so many people, stories, products and memories.

This book and its recipes stem from my two restaurants: The Club and Aqua Kitchen and Bar. It is where most of the photographs were shot and where most of the recipes were developed. In my eyes, the restaurants are ground zero for this book and where everything happens. The staff at both places have so much to do with *Island Kitchen*, they really do help drive me and make everything possible. To me this book is for them, to help further inspire them and share with them my love for Newfoundland food.

Mark McCrowe

Newfoundland is one of the most unique, rugged and breathtaking places on earth. The best way to uncover its raw beauty, sense of history and culture is through its people and their food. Mark has been an ambassador of these great food traditions, mixing old classics with new techniques. Keeping the culinary landscape alive and honest...great chef, good friend...best kind!

Chuck Hughes

Photo courtesy of Darryl Edwards

This book is dedicated to Leo Griffin.
My Poppy, first inspiration and true Newfoundlander.

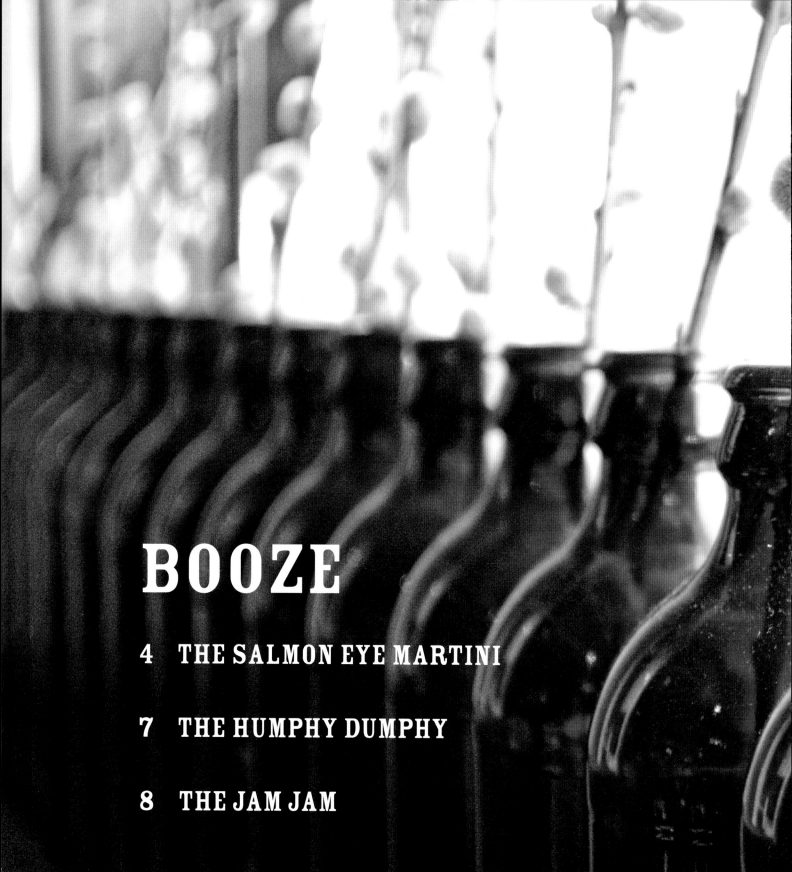

BOOZE

I'm by no means a mixologist but almost every chef has tinkered behind the bar or concocted a drunken masterpiece at some point in time. Here are a couple of Newfie-inspired cocktails that my staff and I have been playing with after hours. Sometimes the misses are as good as the hits!

THE SALMON EYE MARTINI

This recipe is a classic vodka martini recipe using local Iceberg vodka. We garnish with the fresh flavours of cucumber, dill, and smoked salmon. If you're feeling adventurous you can even add the salmon's eye.

Serves: 1

1½ oz Iceberg vodka
¾ oz dry vermouth

GARNISH
Slice of fresh cucumber
1 sprig fresh dill
1 slice of smoked salmon
1 salmon eye
1 lemon twist

Pour the ingredients into a cocktail shaker filled with ice. Shake well. Strain into a chilled cocktail glass.

Garnish with a lemon twist, cucumber slice, fresh dill and a slice of smoked salmon skewered with the salmon's eye.

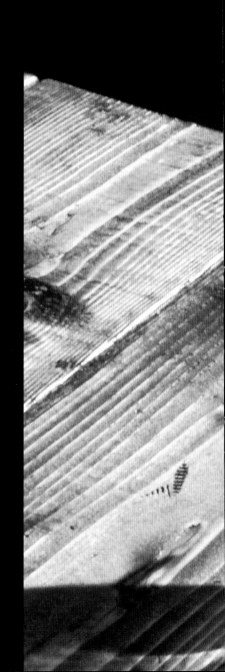

THE HUMPHY DUMPHY

This is a tribute to our buddy Donnie. Pineapple Crush offers an exotic touch that compliments the Screech beautifully.

Serves: 1

2 oz Newfie Screech
Pineapple Crush to taste

On da rocks
Put a few ice cubes into a glass jar. Pour in the Screech and top with Pineapple Crush.

```
How to Be Deadly

1 Part Newfie Screech

1 Part Pineapple Crush

On da rocks!
```

THE JAM JAM

Purity Jam Jams are the quintessential Newfoundland cookie. We created this cocktail to honour its nostalgic flavour.

Serves: 1

½ oz Sailor Jerry spiced rum
½ oz Grand Marnier
¼ oz Butterscotch Ripple
1 oz cranberry juice
1 tsp lemon juice
½ oz Purity raspberry syrup

GARNISH
1 Purity Jam Jam
2 tbsp sugar

Rub the rim of a martini glass with a wedge of lemon and dip into sugar to rim the glass. Put all ingredients into a martini shaker and shake over ice. Pour the mix into your glass and cut a small slit in your cookie to wedge it into the side of the glass.

GIVE US THIS DAY OUR DAILY BREAD

14   NAN'S SWEET ROLLS

15   WHIPPED MOLASSES BUTTER WITH
NEWFOUNDLAND SEA SALT

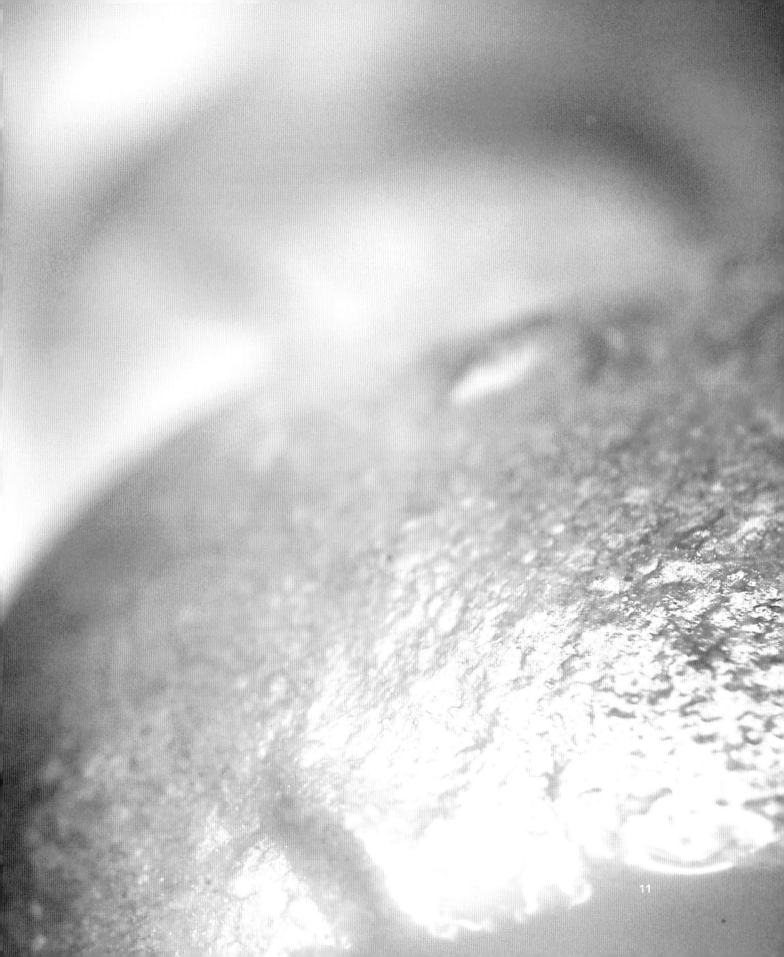

If there is one smell in the world that can put a smile on your face — apart from bacon — it has to be the scent of freshly baked bread coming out of the oven. Growing up my brother and I spent a lot of time with our nan and pop who lived in Long Harbour. Every time we would visit, Nan would have a tub of her cinnamon buns ready to go and every morning we would wake up to her freshly baked bread drizzled with molasses. The bread is unreal and the dough can be used for so many different applications. Whether you want to roll it with butter and sprinkle with cinnamon-sugar to make cinnamon buns, bake it in a loaf or roll it into small buns — the possibilities are endless. It even makes nice pizza dough or a soft pretzel. Every morning at The Club Sasha bakes this recipe for our amazing sweet rolls, burger buns and soft pretzels. Here is the same recipe we use at the restaurant for our sweet rolls with molasses whipped butter — just like Nan's!

us This Day

Daily Bread

NAN'S SWEET ROLLS

Makes: 30 rolls

2 cups warm water
2 cups warm milk
4 eggs
1 ⅓ cups soft butter

1 ⅓ cups white sugar
1 ½ tbsp salt
15 cups all-purpose flour
6 tsp instant yeast
1 cup butter

METHOD

Sift all dry ingredients together in a large mixing bowl. Add eggs and soft butter, mix well. Continue to knead mixture, add warm water and milk until desired consistency is reached. Roll the dough into golf ball-size balls and lay out on a sheet pan lined with parchment paper. Cover with a clean dish towel and allow them to rise for 20-30 minutes. Once the buns have raised, brush them with a little beaten egg and bake at 350°F for 20-30 minutes until golden brown. Allow them to cool on a cooling rack and brush with some melted butter to keep them moist and give them a great shine.

WHIPPED MOLASSES BUTTER WITH NEWFOUNDLAND SEA SALT

This is an amazing way to kick your butter up a notch and it goes so good with Nan's Sweet Rolls. If you can't get your hands on Newfoundland sea salt any other high quality salt will do just fine.

Makes: roughly 1 cup

1 cup unsalted butter, room temperature
3 tbsp fancy molasses
1 pinch of Newfoundland sea salt

METHOD
In a mixer with the whisk attachment, beat all ingredients together for 2-3 minutes until it becomes light and fluffy.

OYSTERS ROCKY HARBOUR

Oysters are not native to Newfoundland but the Maritimes play host to some of the world's finest. We serve them by the dozens at both of my restaurants. They are simple to prepare and are truly a delicacy. There's not much to know when it comes to shucking an oyster. You simply insert your shucker into the back and wiggle it until the shell pops. Once it's popped, run the shucker all the way around the shell to release the abductor muscle. Scrape away any debris from the shell and run your oyster knife under the flesh to release the meat. Give it a good smell. It should smell fresh like the sea – slightly cucumbery and definately not fishy. For me it's simple: if I open one that doesn't smell nice, it goes in the bin. Oysters Rockefeller is a classic oyster dish. The oysters are topped with creamed spinach, bacon and parmesan bread crumbs then broiled until golden brown. It's an amazing dish. Oysters Rocky Harbour is my take on this classic recipe, substituting the spinach for turnip greens, the bacon for salt beef, the butter and parmesan for mornay sauce and the bread crumbs for Mount Scio savoury dressing. It's Oysters Rockefeller with a Newfie twist!

OYSTERS ROCKY HARBOUR

Makes: 12 oysters

FOR THE MORNAY SAUCE
2 tbsp butter
2 tbsp all-purpose flour
2 cups milk
1 tsp salt
 freshly grated nutmeg to taste
¼ cup grated gruyere cheese
¼ cup grated parmesan cheese

In a medium saucepan, heat the butter over medium-low heat until melted. Add the flour and stir until smooth. Over medium heat, cook until the mixture turns a light, golden, sandy colour, about 6 to 7 minutes. Meanwhile, heat the milk in a separate pan until just about boiled. Add the hot milk to the butter mixture 1 cup at a time, whisking continuously until very smooth. Bring to a boil. Cook for 10 minutes, stirring constantly, and then remove from heat. Season with salt and nutmeg, add grated cheese and set aside until ready to use.

FOR THE TURNIP GREENS
2 cups turnip greens (or spinach)
1 tsp olive oil
Salt and freshly cracked black pepper

In a hot pan, sauté the turnip greens with a pinch of salt and cracked black pepper until wilted then set aside.

FOR THE SALT BEEF
1 5-oz chunk of salt beef

Soak the salt beef in cold water overnight in your refrigerator. The next day rinse it well in cold water and simmer in a pot of water for 3 hours until the meat can be easily pulled away from the bone. Cool it down and shred the meat into small strands similar to pulled pork and set aside.

FOR THE SAVOURY DRESSING
1 cup bread crumbs
3 tsp Mount Scio savoury
4 tbsp unsalted butter
½ small white onion, finely diced
Salt and freshly cracked black pepper

In a small pan, sweat the onion in butter until translucent. Add the remaining ingredients and continue to cook for 2 minutes on low heat. Set aside.

TO ASSEMBLE THE OYSTERS ROCKY HARBOUR
Shuck 12 fresh east coast oysters and lay them out on the half shell on a baking tray. Add 1 tsp of the wilted turnip greens to each, then 1 tsp of the pulled salt beef, then spoon 1 tbsp of the mornay sauce to cover the beef and greens. Finally, top each oyster with a generous pinch of savoury dressing and broil in a hot oven until they are golden brown and delicious. Serve them hot, arranged on a bed of sea salt and finish with a squeeze of fresh lemon juice.
(See photo, page 17)

THE DEADLIEST CATCH

We do versions of this dish at both of my restaurants. The idea is simple, whatever fresh seafood you have, either raw or lightly poached, served cold on a bed of ice. You can serve it very simply with just some lemon or you can get more creative and serve it with homemade sauces like a classic mignonette, cocktail sauce or hot sauce. Assembling a seafood platter is very simple, but there are some key things to remember. Always smell your seafood. It should smell fresh like the sea and not fishy. Also, if you have lobster, clams, mussels or shrimp make sure not to overcook them before chilling them down. Other than that the world is your oyster. Put in whatever seafood you like. It's a perfect recipe to bust out for your friends at a dinner party. So simple yet so special at the same time.

REPUBLIC OF SOIL

THE ORGANIC FARM

26 GARDEN SALAD WITH
    BAKEAPPLE AND PORK
    SCRUNCHION VINAIGRETTE

Newfoundland cuisine is based on root vegetables and I have a deeply rooted love for them. Sometimes they are underutilized but can be so versatile if you know how to treat them. We are capable of so much more than just your regular Sunday dinner veg. People on the Island have been really testing the boundaries of what can and can't be grown here over the last number of years. One place in particular deserves full-credit for pioneering how we think about farming in Newfoundland, and through trial and error have totally turned the normal on its head. The Organic Farm is located in Portugal Cove, just a short drive from St. John's. They have been supplying local chefs with the best quality and variety of organically grown vegetables for just about as long as I can remember. They are a real credit to our local food scene and really understand that great ingredients are the real heroes behind a great plate of food. Here is a simple salad that embraces all kinds of beautiful vegetables that can be grown right here on the Island, tied together with the flavour of local bakeapples and the saltiness of pork scrunchions – damn, I can't even make a friggin' salad without adding pork fat.

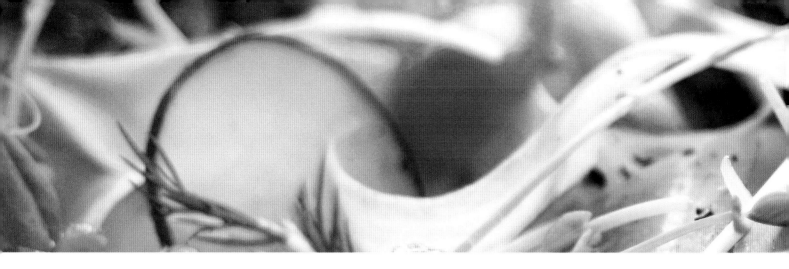

GARDEN SALAD WITH BAKEAPPLE AND PORK SCRUNCHION VINAIGRETTE

Serves: 4

1 head butter lettuce
2 cups baby kale
2 bulbs Belgium endive
1 cup organic pea tendrils
2 heirloom carrots, shaved in ribbons with a vegetable peeler
8 cherry tomatoes, cut in half
1 English cucumber, shaved in ribbons with a vegetable peeler
3 radishes, thinly sliced
½ red onion, thinly sliced
2 sprigs fresh dill

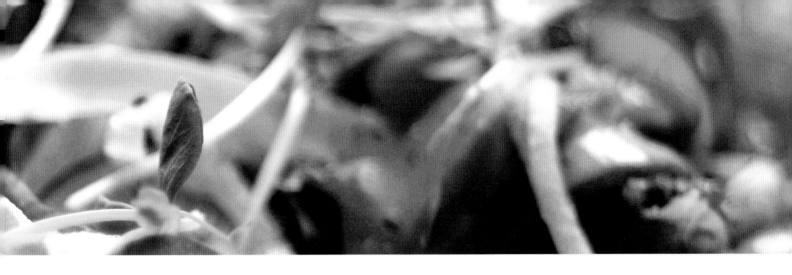

FOR THE SALAD

Wash and prepare all the vegetables and arrange them on a large serving platter. There is no particular right or wrong way – have fun with it!

FOR THE BAKEAPPLE PORK SCRUNCHION VINAIGRETTE

1 cup salt pork fat scrunchions
8 tbsp red wine vinegar
¼ cup bakeapple purée
2 tbsp honey
3 tbsp extra virgin olive oil
Salt and cracked blacked pepper

In a frying pan, render the pork fat scrunchions until golden brown and crispy. Drain them and set aside, reserving 4 tbsp of the rendered pork fat. In a mixing bowl, whisk all of the remaining ingredients together and season with salt and pepper to taste. Add the pork scrunchions and pork fat to finish the dressing. When ready to serve, spoon the vinaigrette over the salad evenly and present to your guests. (See photo, page 25)

FIVE BROTHERS
ARTISAN CHEESE

30 ALMOND CRUSTED
FIVE BROTHERS CHEDDAR

Five Brothers Artisan Cheese was started in March 2011 by owner and cheese-maker Adam Blanchard and it is currently the only cheese producer in Newfoundland and Labrador. Since its beginning, Five Brothers has become a member of the Dairy Farmers of Canada, the Canadian Chefs Federation and the Restaurant Association of Newfoundland. They are also a staunch supporting member of the St. John's Farmers Market. Five Brothers has participated in The Great Canadian Cheese Festival, The Canadian Cheese Grand Prix, Roots Rants & Roars, Eat the Hill and the Savour Food and Wine Show. Five Brothers prides itself on building relationships with producers and chefs in Newfoundland, promoting local foods.

Adam's cheese is awesome. He's a great friend and having a connection with him really makes our food at the restaurants that much more special. Here is a really easy recipe I love to prepare, using Adam's cheese. It's very versatile and can easily be substituted for whatever cheese is available to you.

ALMOND CRUSTED FIVE BROTHERS CHEDDAR

WITH STEWED LOCAL FRUITS IN BIRCH SAP WINE, HONEY GLAZED COUNTRY HAM AND APPLE SALAD

Serves: 4

ALMOND CRUSTED CHEDDAR
4 2-oz wedges of cheddar
1 cup all-purpose flour
2 eggs, lightly beaten
2 cups ground almonds
Salt
Freshly cracked black pepper
8 cups canola oil for frying

STEWED LOCAL FRUITS IN BIRCH SAP WINE
2 cups local fruits of your choice
2 tbsp sugar
1 cup Lady of the Woods birch sap wine

APPLE SALAD
1 Granny Smith apple
½ cup pea tendrils
½ lemon, juiced
2 tbsp extra virgin olive oil
Salt
Freshly cracked black pepper

HONEY GLAZED COUNTRY HAM
4 thick slices of good quality country ham
2 tbsp local honey
Freshly cracked black pepper

FOR THE STEWED FRUIT

Combine the fruits with the sugar in a small saucepan over medium-high heat, until sugar is melted and slightly caramelized. Deglaze with the birch sap wine and reduce the heat to a simmer, until the sauce becomes slightly thick but still thin enough to act as a fruit syrup.

FOR THE GLAZED HAM

Slice 4 generous pieces of country-style ham and lay them out on a cookie sheet lined with parchment paper. Brush each slice with honey and season with cracked black pepper. Bake in a 350°F oven until the honey has glazed on nicely. About 20 minutes.

FOR THE APPLE SALAD

Slice the apple in a thin julienne cut using a sharp knife or slicing mandolin, drizzle with the lemon juice and olive oil. Toss in the pea sprouts and season with salt and pepper. It's important to do the apples just before plating the dish, because once they are sliced they tend to wilt and discolour.

FOR THE CHEESE

Set up three plates: one with flour, one with egg wash and the last one with ground almonds. Make sure to season the flour with salt and pepper. In the meantime, set the deep fryer with canola oil to 375°F . Bread each piece of cheese by first putting in the flour, then the egg wash and finally into the ground almonds. When all four pieces are done, fry them in the hot oil until light golden brown. Drain on a paper towel. Arrange four bowls and spoon some of the stewed fruit in the bottom of each bowl. Then place your cheese in each bowl, resting the glazed ham slice up against the side of the cheese. Top each piece of cheese with some apple salad and drizzle some extra virgin olive oil around the bowl for extra flavour.

THE CAPELIN ROLL

34 TEMPURA CAPELIN WITH DYNAMITE
SAUCE, PICKLED CARROT, CUCUMBER,
SESAME AND WASABI- SOY

The capelin or caplin (Mallotus villosus), is a small forage fish of the smelt family that can be found in the Atlantic and Arctic oceans. In the summer, it grazes on dense swarms of plankton at the edge of the ice shelf. Larger capelin also eat a great deal of krill and other crustaceans. Capelin gather to mate near beaches, and waves roll them onto the pebbles by the hundreds. Battered and exhausted after spawning, many don't make it back to sea. The capelin scull draws a mix of predators into shore: whales, cod, and puffins all join in the feast. People cast and dip their nets, filling their buckets by literally scooping them from the waves as they tumble ashore. When I think of capelin I think of sardines and treat them very simply, usually pan seared in pork scrunchions and olive oil with some fresh lemon and arugula. Here is a fun little take on capelin with a Japanese twist.

TEMPURA CAPELIN WITH DYNAMITE SAUCE, PICKLED CARROT, CUCUMBER, SESAME AND WASABI-SOY

Serves: 2

FOR THE DYNAMITE SAUCE
4 tbsp mayo
4 tbsp sriracha chili sauce

Mix the mayo and the chili sauce together till nice and smooth.

FOR THE PICKLED CARROT AND CUCUMBER
1 English cucumber
1 carrot
2 cups rice wine vinegar
4 tbsp sugar
2 tsp salt
2 star anise pods

Peel the carrot and cucumber, then continue peeling them to form nice little noodle-shaped ribbons. Boil the vinegar, sugar, salt and star anise until sugar is dissolved, then chill. Once the pickling liquid is chilled, pour over the vegetables and let it sit for at least 2 hours to pickle.

FOR THE SESAME WASABI–SOY
4 tbsp soy sauce
1 pinch of wasabi powder
2 drops of sesame oil
1 tsp honey

Whisk all ingredients together.

FOR THE TEMPURA CAPELIN
10 fresh capelin
1 cup all-purpose flour
1 tbsp cornstarch
1 ½ cups club soda
Pinch of salt
Pinch of Chinese five-spice
2 litres canola oil for frying

Preheat the canola oil to 350°F in a household deep fryer. Rinse the capelin in cold water, pat dry and set aside. Mix all the other ingredients together in a bowl to form the tempura batter. Dip each capelin into the batter and gently drop into the hot oil, until lightly golden brown. While still hot, season with salt. Spread some dynamite sauce on the bottom of a plate, lay out five capelin per person and drape some of the pickled vegetables on top. Drizzle with the wasabi-soy and garnish with sesame seeds and organic pea tendrils.

MUDDER'S PICKLES

39 THE PICKLES

his is a super traditional family recipe and we use it as a condiment for our savory cod cakes at the restaurant. It is really easy to make at home especially when you mother or "mudder" is the one making it! It's also a killer condiment to eat with Jiggs dinner. When it's mixed with salt beef and pease pudding, you can't beat it!

Makes: approximately 12 servings

THE PICKLES
¼ cup salt
2 cups sugar
1 cup vinegar
1 red pepper
2 cups onion
2 English cucumbers
1 tbsp mustard powder
1 500ml bottle yellow mustard
1 tbsp corn starch, mixed into slurry
1 tsp turmeric
1 head cauliflower
½ head cabbage
1 green pepper

METHOD
Roughly chop the vegetables and combine all ingredients into a large heavy-bottomed pot. Bring to a boil and reduce the heat to a simmer. Cook for about 20 minutes and stir occasionally to make sure it doesn't stick. Let cool and serve at room temperature.

SALT BEEF JUNKIE

42 JIGGS DINNER CROQUETTES WITH MUDDER'S PICKLES

"SALT BEEF JUNKIE"

God bless my soul what can I do they say my salt beef dinner is a killer
It's got carcinogens and heavy duty fats it could serve as an elephant filler.
I'm as good as dead but I'm sure well fed 'cause I love those buckets of riblets
I love to drink that liquor and chew those bones even though I'm picking my giblets

Chorus:
Put on the beef, peas pudding and the greens
Carrots and turnips, can't you smell that steam
Some new potatoes with a puddin' good and lumpy
No I just can't wait, I'm a salt beef junkie.

Now some folks like to eat carrot sticks 'cause they're afraid they might become gluttons,
But me I don't like those rabbit foods 'cause I'm afraid that I might pass buttons
Every Sunday morning while some folks fast or eat food that tastes real crappy
I got my salt beef dinner cooking on the stove 'cause I wanna die real happy.
Jane Fonda likes to eat sesame seeds and Twiggy likes low fat tofu
But they don't live in Newfoundland where the winter winds blow right through you
Now if they lived in Wesleyville where the north wind blows right vicious
They'd enjoy their salt beef dinners just like me and the missus
I don't want to be some health food freak who eats alfalfa and bean sprouts
I don't want to live to a hundred and three if I got to throw my beef out
When it comes right down to preparing food I don't want to germinate or shuck it
I'll take my chances on salt beef dinners and keep my head in this bucket.

Recorded by: Buddy Wasisname and the Other Fellers
Written by: Wayne Chaulk

This appetizer packs all the punch of a plate of Jiggs dinner in a bite-sized golden brown ball of deliciousness. At the restaurant we serve them with my nan's mustard pickle recipe or as we call them, "Mudder's Pickles."

JIGGS DINNER CROQUETTES WITH MUDDER'S PICKLES

Makes: 20 croquettes

FOR THE CROQUETTE MIX
2 large russet potatoes, peeled
1 cup turnip, roughly chopped
1 cup green cabbage, roughly chopped
1 carrot, peeled and roughly chopped
1 8-oz chunk of salt beef
1 cup yellow split peas, soaked overnight

In a large pot, simmer the salt beef in water for 2 hours, add all of the other ingredients and top up the pot with water to cover vegetables. Continue to simmer until the vegetables are fork-tender. Drain the ingredients very well in a colander. Remove the salt beef and shred the meat into small strands, then put with the vegetables and mash everything until the whole mix is even. Place in refrigerator for 30 minutes to help the mix firm up. Then roll them into bite-size balls and put back in the fridge until ready to bread.

(See photo, page 40)

FOR THE BREADING
4 cups all-purpose flour
5 eggs, beaten
6 cups panko bread crumbs
2 litres canola oil for frying
Salt to season

Preheat the canola oil to 350°F in a household deep fryer. In three different bowls separate the flour, eggs and the bread crumbs. Start by rolling each croquette first in the flour, then in the egg wash and then finally into the panko bread crumbs. When all of the croquettes have been breaded, fry them in small batches of about 5 or 6 until golden brown. Season with salt while they are still hot and serve with Mudder's Pickles (recipe found on page 39.)

LET'S GO TO THE PLATE

Behind the scenes in a restaurant is a very different setting than what you see in the dining room. If you're in an establishment of quality you probably have a highly trained group of cooks that have been working together day-in and day-out for many years. The kitchen has to have a rhythm to it and needs to work in sync with the front of house to get the food to the diner in a timely fashion. Every job is as important as the next and it all factors in to how the customer enjoys their dining experience. The chef of a restaurant has to control every aspect of the kitchen, from ordering the vegetables and meats, to scheduling staff, to coming up with daily specials, to prepping all the food for service and making sure all the cooks are carrying out their jobs as expected. That's if you live in a perfect world. So many things can go wrong in a restaurant kitchen, from an over-flowing grease trap, products not showing up on time, hungover staff, to having to play guidance counselor to another cook who

just broke-up with his girlfriend. You have to expect anything and everything. In many cases the kitchen staff is small and being able to bang out fifty covers with a brigade of 2-3 people is sometimes an uphill battle. This is why organization is so important in a professional kitchen. Everything must be ready to go and when it's time to plate food, it must be perfect. Everything on the plate must be how it was intended to be. If a piece of fish is overcooked it makes more sense to throw it out and start fresh rather than send it to a paying customer and either have them make you cook it again or not return to your restaurant. There's an old saying, "never let your mistakes leave the kitchen," and I believe if you can pull that off and offer great service your restaurant is on the right track. When you can get a group of people together that share a passion for food and you are blessed with being able to work with great ingredients, the possibilities are endless. A well-oiled kitchen is a thing of beauty and it really takes a special group of people to make magic happen night after night. Here's to all the hard-working cooks, servers, bus boys and dishwashers all over the world that run and work in restaurants. They truly should be celebrated as much as possible.

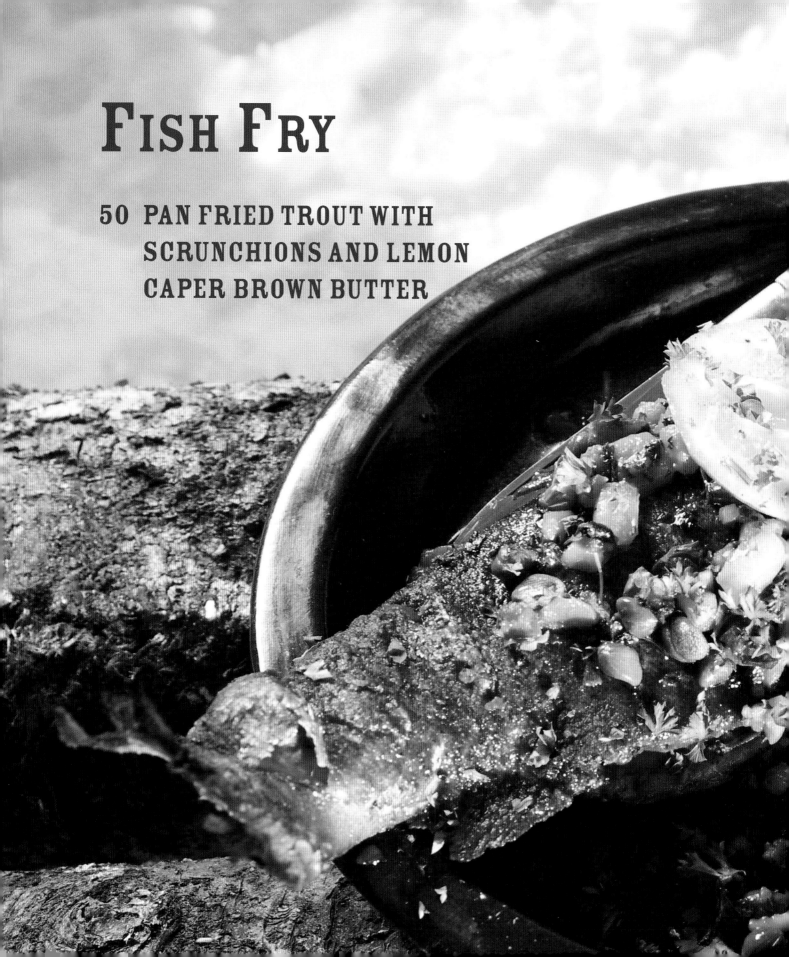

FISH FRY

50 PAN FRIED TROUT WITH
    SCRUNCHIONS AND LEMON
    CAPER BROWN BUTTER

Whether I'm fishing in the summer on a camping trip with my buds or I'm out on a cold lake ice fishing in the winter, I always bring a frying pan. There are no words to describe the feeling of popping a fish right out of the water and into a hot frying pan. I like it simple with just a little dusting of flour, salt and pepper and fried up crispy in some sizzling butter. In this recipe I even went as far as to fry up pork scrunchions, capers, parsley and fresh lemon juice – I think it's a new standard.

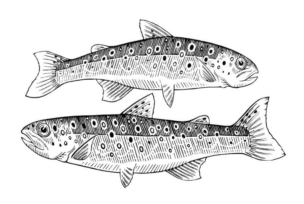

PAN FRIED TROUT WITH SCRUNCHIONS AND LEMON CAPER BROWN BUTTER

This can easily be done at home but the secret ingredient is cooking it over an open fire with your friends. The cooking time of the trout really depends on how big it is. Don't be afraid to poke a knife through the flesh to check the doneness. I like mine a little pink but feel free to cook it more or less to your taste.

Serves: 2-4 hungry people

PAN FRIED TROUT
2 super fresh trout, cleaned and gutted
1 cup all-purpose flour
Salt and freshly cracked black pepper
4 tbsp unsalted butter

SCRUNCHIONS AND LEMON CAPER BROWN BUTTER SAUCE
1 cup salt pork fat, roughly chopped
1 lemon, sliced into quarters
4 tbsp capers, plus 1 tbsp of juice

6 tbsp chopped parsley
5 tbsp unsalted butter

FOR THE TROUT

Preheat a non stick frying pan that is big enough to accommodate your trout to medium heat. In the meantime, season your fish with salt and freshly cracked black pepper. Coat each side of the fish with a light coating of all-purpose flour and set aside. Melt the butter in the pan until it gets nice and toasty and then gently place your fish in, laying it away from you so you don't get any splash back from the butter. Allow your fish to cook for about 10 minutes per side. It should be golden and crispy. Check the inside to make sure it's cooked through by poking a knife through the flesh. It should be slightly pink but not raw. Set your fish aside to rest and save your pan to create the sauce.

FOR THE SCRUNCHION BROWN BUTTER SAUCE

In the same pan that you fried the trout, add all the scrunchions and cook over a medium heat until they are lightly golden brown and the fat is rendered. Drain the excess fat and set aside the scrunchions to be added back into the sauce at the end. Add the butter to the pan and allow it to cook until it becomes a rich golden brown colour. It's important not to burn it, but take it to a really nutty colour. Once you reach that colour, squeeze the lemon quarters into the pan and toss the pieces in to stew with the sauce. Add the capers and juice, and then the chopped parsley. Cook for another 30-40 seconds then toss in the rendered pork scrunchions. While the sauce is hot, spoon it over your trout and tuck in before it gets cold! (See photo, page 46)

O TOUTON! MY TOUTON!

Toutons are the quintessential Newfoundland recipe. They are literally fried bread dough. You can fry them in oil, butter, pork fat or even duck fat. It's really up to you. Toutons drizzled with molasses is the classic way of serving them, but at the restaurants we like to have a little fun by topping them with some of our favourite flavours. Toutons with smoked salmon, capers and onion, touton breakfast sandwiches and toutons with Korean-style pork and pickles are some of our favourites. We even make stuffed toutons with bakeapple whipped cream for dessert. Here are two of our favourite ways to have a little fun with toutons that you can make at home.

FRIED TOUTON FILLED WITH BAKEAPPLE CHANTILLY CREAM AND BERRY JAM

This is a great way to dress up a simple touton. You can cut them in half and stuff them with literally anything under the moon. In this recipe we filled them with bakeapple whipped cream and a local berry jam but feel free to add your favourite dessert flavours. Strawberry shortcake, bananas and nutella and stewed apples with maple syrup and vanilla ice cream are some of my favourites.

Serves: 4

FOR THE TOUTON
1 batch of Nan's Sweet Roll dough (recipe on page 14)

Once you have your bread dough mixed and rested, roll some of it out on a sheet to about 1-inch thick. Use a round cookie cutter and cut out rounds of the dough. Preheat a cast iron pan and melt about 2 tbsp of butter. Once the butter begins to sizzle, add the toutons and fry until golden brown on both sides. Set them aside to cool slightly before filling them.

FOR THE BAKEAPPLE PURÉE
2 cups bakeapples
½ cup sugar

In a small saucepan, simmer the berries with the sugar on a medium-low heat for 10-15 minutes. Pass the sauce through a fine mesh strainer and chill in the fridge.

FOR THE BAKEAPPLE CHANTILLY CREAM
1 cup heavy whipping cream
2 tbsp icing sugar
Vanilla extract, to taste
4 tbsp bakeapple purée

In an electric mixer with the whisk attachment, whisk together the cream, sugar and vanilla, until the cream becomes stiff and sticks to the back of a spoon. Gently stir in the chilled bakeapple purée and place in a piping bag or a sandwich bag with the corner cut off.

FOR THE BERRY JAM
½ cup blueberries
½ cup partridgeberries
½ cup strawberries
½ cup sugar

In a small saucepan, simmer the berries with the sugar on a medium-low heat for 10-15 minutes, until thick and jammy. Cool down and reserve in the fridge until needed.

TO ASSEMBLE THE TOUTONS
Cut the touton in half with a bread knife. Pipe the bakeapple whipped cream to cover the bottom touton then spoon the berry jam over the top, try to cover evenly. Garnish the plate with some bakeapple purée and whipped cream. Dust the touton with icing sugar and place on the plate with some edible flowers to make it extra pretty. (See photo, page 53)

KOREAN-STYLE PORK BUNS WITH FRIED TOUTONS, PICKLES AND HOISIN-MOLASSES

This recipe is basically our rendition of the highly popular Korean-style pork buns, made famous by David Chang of the Momofuku restaurants. In this recipe, instead of steaming the buns we lightly fry them in butter to give them that touton feel.

Serves: 4

FOR THE TOUTON BUNS
1 batch of Nan's Sweet Roll dough (recipe on page 14)

Once you have your bread dough mixed and rested, simply divide some of the dough into little golf ball-sized balls. Once they are formed, cover them and allow them to rest for approximately 15 minutes. Finally, roll the dough balls out into oval shapes with a rolling pin or wine bottle. Preheat a cast iron pan and melt about 2 tbsp of butter. Once the butter begins to sizzle, add the toutons and fry till golden brown on both sides.

FOR THE ROASTED PORK BELLY
2 lbs pork belly	**Freshly cracked black peppercorns**
Sea salt	**Chinese five-spice**

Take your pork belly and season it generously on both sides with the salt, pepper and five-spice. Place it on a roasting rack covered with tinfoil and cook it low and slow at 350°F for 2-3 hours. During the last 30 minutes or so of cooking remove the tinfoil and allow the skin to become golden brown and crispy. Once cooked, allow the meat to rest and slice into thick slabs, to approximately the same thickness as the touton buns.

FOR THE PICKLES
1 English cucumber
1 carrot
2 tbsp sugar
1 tsp salt
6 tbsp rice wine vinegar
1 star anise

Slice the cucumber into thin circles. Shave the carrot into long ribbons, using a vegetable peeler. Sprinkle all the remaining ingredients over the vegetables and refrigerate for at least 2 hours or overnight if you have the time.

FOR THE HOISIN-MOLASSES
1 cup hoisin sauce
1 cup molasses

Mix both ingredients together until combined.

TO ASSEMBLE THE BUNS
Brush each touton with the molasses hoisin sauce and top with a slice of the roasted pork belly and a couple of slices of carrot and cucumber. For additional garnish add some sliced green onion, crushed peanuts and black and white sesame seeds. Serve hot with a side of sriracha chili sauce.

NEWFOUNDLAND DUCK COMPANY

60 BLACK PEPPER AND HONEY GLAZED
NL DUCK BREAST WITH NEWMAN'S
PORT AND WILD BLUEBERRY REDUCTION

Based out of Grand Falls-Windsor, The Newfoundland Duck Company is rearing some of the most amazing duck you can get your hands on. They also raise quail and have a large supply of quail eggs and berries. Here is a simple recipe using Newfoundland duck and local blueberries. Newman's Port helps fortify the sauce and add a super-rich flavour.

BLACK PEPPER AND HONEY GLAZED NL DUCK BREAST WITH NEWMAN'S PORT AND WILD BLUEBERRY REDUCTION

Serves: 2

FOR THE DUCK
2 large duck breasts
Salt and freshly cracked black pepper
2 tbsp honey

Score the duck skin with a sharp knife in a crosshatch pattern while making sure not to slice through the meat. This will keep the duck from curling up while cooking. Season generously with salt and freshly cracked black pepper. Put it in a cold pan over a medium heat skin side down and slowly render the fat until it becomes golden and crispy, roughly 10 minutes. When golden and crispy drain off the excess fat and reserve for another use. Turn the duck and cook on the other side for another 2 minutes or so. Spoon the honey over and take the duck out of the pan to let it rest.

FOR THE PORT AND BLUEBERRY SAUCE
¼ cup wild blueberries
1 tbsp honey
1 sprig thyme
½ shallot, finely diced
1 cup Newman's Port
1 tbsp unsalted butter
Salt and freshly cracked black pepper

In the same pan as the duck was cooked, add the honey and shallots. Cook for 1-2 minutes on a medium-high heat and deglaze with the port. Add the thyme, salt and pepper, reduce until it becomes a sauce consistency. Just before serving the sauce, take it off the heat and whisk in 1 tbsp of cold butter. This will help make the sauce more luscious and shiny. Slice the duck on a slight angle and fan it out on a plate, then spoon the sauce over and around the plate. Serve with your favourite seasonal vegetables.

(See photo, page 58)

FRESH OFF DA BOAT

64   LEMON PEPPER SMOKED COD AND
CRISPY BRITCHES WITH MINT, LEMON
AND GREEN PEA RISOTTO

66   SNOW CRAB AND SEA URCHIN PANNA
COTTA WITH MAPLE GLAZED PORK BELLY

68   CORNMEAL FRIED COD TONGUE AND
CHEEK WITH GREEN OLIVE, APPLE,
RAISIN AND MINT SALSA

70   NL SEAFOOD CHOWDER WITH ROASTED
FENNEL, DILL AND EVAPORATED MILK

72   HALLIDAY'S BLOOD PUDDING AND
LOBSTER STUFFED SQUID WITH BISQUE
SAUCE

There is such a variety of seafood that comes from the Atlantic Ocean. It's a sin that most of the time we don't even have access to it. Most products get shipped off to foreign markets leaving us with a few staples that, to a chef, can become very boring . However, if you keep your eye out and become well connected with suppliers and fishermen, you can really discover some great products. One advantage of having a limited variety of fish is that we really learn to use all the parts. From their innards to their tongues and cheeks nothing gets wasted. Here are a few seafood dishes that are really simple, super tasty and very regional.

LEMON PEPPER SMOKED COD AND CRISPY BRITCHES WITH MINT, LEMON AND GREEN PEA RISOTTO

Cod britches are the roe sac of a female cod and are named for their resemblance to a pair of baggy trousers. In this dish, we smoke cod loin with lemon zest and cracked pepper, fry the cod britches until crispy and serve it over a creamy mint and pea risotto. So good!

Serves: 4

FOR THE LEMON PEPPER SMOKED COD
1 8-oz cod loin
1 lemon, zested   Cracked black pepper
Sea salt   1 cup woodchips, soaked in water

To smoke the cod loins put the woodchips in the bottom of a frying pan or wok and put it over a burner on medium heat. Once it starts to smoke, take the cod loin and sprinkle it with the lemon zest and cracked black pepper. Place on a rack that can fit in the frying pan. By this time there should be quite a bit of smoke so you want to cover it tightly with tinfoil to capture all that smoke. Let them go for about 10-12 minutes then take them off the heat. The cod should be flakey and cooked through.

FOR THE CRISPY BRITCHES   Freshly cracked black pepper
2 cod britches, cut into small pieces   1 cup all-purpose flour
Sea salt   Canola oil for frying

Season the cod britches and dust them in the flour, shaking off any excess. Fry them in a household deep fryer set at 375°F until golden brown. Drain on paper towel and season again with sea salt.

FOR THE MINT, LEMON AND GREEN PEA RISOTTO
5 to 6 cups fish stock
4 tbsp unsalted butter
1 onion, finely diced
Sea salt
2 cups Arborio rice
½ cup dry white wine

2 cups frozen peas
⅓ cup chopped fresh mint
2 tbsp fresh lemon juice
1 tbsp lemon zest, finely grated
¼ cup Parmigiano Reggiano, freshly grated

Heat the fish stock in a saucepan over medium-high heat until hot and then reduce the heat to keep the broth hot. In another heavy saucepan, melt 2 tbsp of the butter over medium heat. Add the onion and a generous pinch of salt and sauté, stirring occasionally with a wooden spoon, until the onion softens and starts to turn lightly golden, 3-5 minutes. Add the rice and stir until the grains are well coated with butter and the edges become translucent, approximately 1-2 minutes. Pour in the wine and stir until it's absorbed, about 1 minute. Add another generous pinch of salt and ladle enough of the hot broth into the pan to barely cover the rice, about 1 cup. Bring to a boil and then adjust the heat to maintain a lively simmer. Stirring occasionally, cook until the stock has been mostly absorbed, about 2-3 minutes. Continue adding broth in ½ cup increments, stirring and simmering, until it has been absorbed each time, at intervals of about 2-3 minutes. After about 16-18 minutes the rice should be creamy but still fairly firm. At this point, add the peas and another ½ cup of broth. Continue to simmer and stir until the peas are just cooked and the rice is just tender to the tooth, another 3-4 minutes. Stir in another splash of broth if the risotto is too thick. Remove the pot from the heat and stir in the mint, lemon juice, lemon zest, the remaining 2 tbsp butter, and the Parmigiano. Season with salt to taste. Serve the risotto immediately with a sprinkling of chopped mint and grated lemon zest. Top with some crispy britches, flakes of the smoked cod loin and 'Bob's your uncle.' (See photo, page 63)

SNOW CRAB AND SEA URCHIN PANNA COTTA WITH MAPLE GLAZED PORK BELLY

Sea urchin is the essence of the sea. This silky panna cotta recipe carries these flavours beautifully and the sweet snow crab and maple glazed pork belly turn this dish from elegant to extravagant.

Serves: 4

FOR THE SEA URCHIN PANNA COTTA
2 tbsp cold water
1 tsp gelatin powder
2 cups heavy cream
3 tbsp sea urchin roe
4 oz snow crab meat

In a small bowl, combine the water and gelatin and let soak about 10 minutes (do not stir). Meanwhile, in a medium saucepan, heat the cream to a simmer over medium heat. As soon as it simmers, turn off the heat and add the gelatin mixture and the sea urchin roe, stirring until the gelatin is dissolved. Strain the mixture and pour into 4 tea cups with 1 oz of the snow crab meat in the bottom of each cup. Chill uncovered for 2 hours.

FOR THE MAPLE GLAZED PORK BELLY
1 8-oz piece of pork belly
Sea salt
Cracked black pepper
2 oz Quebec maple syrup

Season the pork and slow roast at 350°F for roughly 2 hours. During the last 30 minutes of cooking glaze with the maple syrup. When the meat has cooled slice into 4 pieces to be placed on top of each panna cotta.

TO GARNISH THE DISH
2 oz snow crab meat
4 tsp sea urchin roe
Organic edible flowers

Top each panna cotta with a little extra snow crab, sea urchin and the maple glazed pork belly. If you can get your hands on some organic edible flowers use them to pretty up the dish.

CORNMEAL FRIED COD TONGUE AND CHEEK WITH GREEN OLIVE, APPLE, RAISIN AND MINT SALSA

This dish has been a staple at Aqua forever. I love the crispy cornmeal crust on the cod along with the salty, sweetness of the salsa. We use a sumac yogurt to round out the dish.

Serves: 4

FOR THE COD TONGUES AND CHEEKS
16 cod tongues
16 cod cheeks
1 cup all-purpose flour
1 cup yellow cornmeal
Sea salt
Cracked black pepper
5 tbsp olive oil

Season the cod tongues and cheeks and dust in a mixture of flour and cornmeal. Heat a large non-stick frying pan over medium-high heat and fry the cod for roughly 2 minutes on each side or until nice and golden brown.

FOR THE GREEN OLIVE SALSA
20 green olives, diced
1 green apple, peeled and diced
½ cup raisins
½ shallot, diced
2 tbsp fresh mint, chopped
2 tbsp sherry vinegar
Pinch of cumin
¼ cup extra virgin olive oil
2 tbsp capers

FOR THE SUMAC YOGURT
½ cup yogurt
Pinch of sumac
Pinch of salt

Mix together in a bowl and set aside.

NL SEAFOOD CHOWDER WITH ROASTED FENNEL, DILL AND EVAPORATED MILK

This chowder is a canvas to show off some of the Rock's best seafood. You can use whatever you have available in this recipe. The flavors of roasted fennel, dill and lemon really make it special and by using evaporated milk you really get that authentic chowder flavour.

Makes: 10-12 portions

FOR THE CHOWDER
½ cup unsalted butter
½ cup all-purpose flour
1 onion, diced
2 stalks celery, diced
2 heads fennel, diced
2 potatoes, diced
¼ cup Pernod
1 cup dry white wine
1 litre fish stock
½ litre heavy cream
2 cans evaporated milk

½ cup chopped dill
5 tbsp lemon juice
3 dashes Tabasco sauce
3 dashes Worcestershire sauce
Salt
Cracked black pepper
1 cup cold water shrimp, peeled
1 lb fresh cod
½ lb mussels
½ lb clams
1 lb cooked lobster meat
½ lb cooked snow crab meat

On a large roasting tray, mix the diced fennel with 4 tbsp of olive oil, salt and pepper. Roast in a 400°F oven until lightly caramelized. In a large heavy-bottomed pot, melt the butter and flour together forming a roux, cook for 2 minutes. Add all of the vegetables and cook them for roughly 5 minutes or until translucent. Add the roasted fennel and deglaze the pot with the pernod and white wine while stirring constantly. Add the remaining liquids and bring to a boil, reducing to a simmer and cook slowly for roughly 30 minutes or until the vegetables are soft and the soup has slightly thickened. Season with salt and pepper then add all the seafood and cook for just a couple of minutes. In a separate pan cook the mussels and clams with 2 cups of the chowder base until the shells open, then add them back into the main pot. At the last minute before serving add the fresh dill and adjust the seasoning to your taste.

HALLIDAY'S BLOOD PUDDING AND LOBSTER STUFFED SQUID WITH BISQUE SAUCE

Halliday's Meat Market is a stone's throw away from my restaurants and they have been supplying us with some of the most amazing blood puddings around. This dish is all about lobster, blood pudding and squid. Super rich and super delish.

Serves: 4

FOR THE STUFFED SQUID
2 large squid tubes
2 blood puddings
4 oz cooked lobster meat

With a knife slice the blood puddings in half, lengthwise and crumble the filling into a bowl, discarding the casing. Add the cooked lobster meat and mix thoroughly. Stuff the mixture inside the cleaned squid tubes until they are about three-quarters full. Use a toothpick to skewer the end together so the filling doesn't pour out during cooking. Drizzle the stuffed squids with a little olive oil and season with salt and pepper. Place on a roasting pan and cook the squid in a 400°F oven for roughly 20 minutes. When they come out of the oven allow them to cool slightly. Remove the toothpicks and slice into ½-inch slices.

FOR THE LOBSTER BISQUE SAUCE

Lobster broth
1 tbsp unsalted butter
1 tbsp extra virgin olive oil
2 red onions, roughly chopped
3 carrots, roughly chopped
2 ribs celery, roughly chopped
6 garlic cloves, smashed
½ tsp sea salt
Cracked black pepper
2 oz brandy
1 cup dry white wine
6 cups fish stock
⅓ cup tomato paste
1 handful parsley
1 sprig thyme

2 bay leaves
3 cooked lobster carcasses, chopped
Water

Dark roux
½ cup unsalted butter
½ cup all-purpose flour

Lobster bisque
1 cup heavy cream
½ tsp saffron

Lobster garnish
3 cooked lobster, meat only
2 tbsp unsalted butter

Heat a large soup pot on medium and add butter, olive oil, onions, carrots, celery and garlic. Add sea salt and freshly cracked black pepper and sauté for about 8 minutes. Deglaze the pan with brandy and burn off the alcohol. Pour in the white wine, and reduce for 1-2 minutes. Add fish stock, tomato paste, parsley, thyme, bay leaves and lobster carcasses (keep meat for later). Top off with water, just enough to cover shells. Turn heat down to medium-low and simmer partially covered for 1 hour.

Dark Roux
Heat a small saucepan on medium. Add butter and flour and whisk continuously for 6-7 minutes, until amber in colour and nutty smelling. Remove from heat.

Lobster Bisque
Using strainer and cheesecloth, strain broth into a medium pot. Add dark roux, heavy cream, and saffron, then mix. Let reduce on medium-low heat for another 15-20 minutes, until thick.

Lobster Garnish
Heat a big pan on medium-high and melt butter. Add lobster meat and sauté for 1-2 minutes, until heated through.

Gotta Get
Me Moose B'y

Eating the heart of a beast has a very primal feel to it and the heart of a moose is actually quite delicious. All the same, it's not something that is readily available, so you can easily make this recipe with a nice chunk of moose roast or steak. The heart stuffed with dressing and gravy is the first way I ate it and this recipe is homage to simple preparation.

STUFFED MOOSE HEART D AND G WITH POMMES FRITES, MUSHY PEAS AND MALT SPRITZER

Serves: 4 hungry humans

FOR THE MOOSE HEART
1 moose heart
1 cup savoury dressing (Recipe on page 19)
Fresh rosemary
Fresh thyme
Fresh parsley
2 cloves garlic
Sea salt
Cracked black pepper
2 tbsp olive oil

Trim the moose heart of fat and sinew. Butterfly the heart into a flat shape so you can place all of the dressing inside and roll the heart in a roulade fashion. Tie the heart with butchers twine so it doesn't unfold during roasting. Season with salt and cracked black pepper. Rub with the chopped herbs and garlic, drizzle with olive oil. Place the moose in a 400°F oven for roughly 1 hour depending on the size. The goal is to keep the meat slightly pink and juicy.
(Recipe continued on page 78)

FOR THE BONE MARROW GRAVY
2-3 beef bones with marrow
2 shallots, chopped
2 tbsp butter
1 tbsp brown sugar
1 cup Bordeaux red wine
1 sprig fresh thyme
1 cup homemade or store bought demi-glace
1 tbsp cognac
2 tbsp chopped parsley
Sea salt and cracked black pepper

Remove the bone marrow. To do this, press the marrow with your thumb to push it out of the bones. If the marrow is stuck, warm the bones in a 350°F preheated oven for 8-10 minutes and press again. If necessary, remove with a small knife. Cut the marrow into ½-inch thick slices, set aside. In a small saucepan, soften the shallots in the butter, add sugar and cook for 1 minute. Deglaze with the wine and add thyme. Bring to a boil and reduce by half, about 10 minutes. Add the demi-glace and bring to a boil. Simmer for about 10 minutes or until the sauce is syrupy. Add the cognac and remove the thyme. Season with salt and cracked black pepper, set aside. In a skillet over high heat, quickly brown the marrow on each side. Deglaze the skillet with the sauce and heat gently until the marrow is cooked. Add the parsley and adjust the seasoning to your taste.

FOR THE POMMES FRITES
4 large russet potatoes
Sea salt
4 cups canola oil for frying

Peel potatoes and cut lengthwise into sticks, about ⅓-inch thick, transferring them into a bowl of cold water as you work. Drain and rinse, until water runs clear. Pat dry with paper towels. Heat oil in a 14-inch straight-sided skillet until oil registers 275°F on a deep-fry thermometer. Add half of the potatoes and distribute evenly. Cook without stirring, until barely golden, 2-3 minutes. Using a slotted spoon, transfer to a baking sheet lined with paper towels to drain. Repeat with remaining potatoes. Preheat oil to 375°F and once again fry the potatoes until golden brown and crispy. Season with salt and serve immediately.

FOR THE MUSHY PEAS
2 tbsp olive oil
2 spring onions, chopped
1 sprig fresh mint leaves, chopped
2 cups frozen green peas
2 tbsp butter

Heat the oil in a pan and add the chopped onions, mint and peas. Cover and leave for a few minutes to steam. Place everything in a food processor and pulse until smooth. Add the butter and season to taste.

FOR THE MALT SPRITZER
Fill a small spritzer bottle with malt vinegar to give an even mist of vinegar on your fries.

Moose tenderloin or "filet mignon" is the most prized cut of the moose. Like beef tenderloin it's super lean and super tender. The key here is to wrap it in bacon to help keep it moist. We also marinate the meat and cook it to a medium-rare. This is truly the ultimate way to experience moose.

BACON WRAPPED FILET MIGNON WITH ROASTED GARLIC MASHED POTATOES, ROASTED BEETS, SPINACH AND PAN JUS

Serves: 4 lucky bastards

FOR THE MOOSE TENDERLOIN AND JUS
4 8-oz portions of moose tenderloin
4 strips bacon
4 cloves garlic, roughly chopped
2 sprigs fresh rosemary
2 tbsp olive oil
Sea salt
Cracked black pepper
1 shallot, chopped
1 cup red wine
1 tsp Dijon mustard
½ cup moose or beef stock
1 tbsp butter

(Recipe continued on page 82)

Wrap the moose tenderloin portions with bacon and secure the end piece with a toothpick so the bacon does not unravel during cooking. Sprinkle with the chopped garlic and rosemary and drizzle with olive oil. Just before cooking, season with salt and pepper. In a hot cast iron pan, sear the steak on all sides and continue to cook until you reach a nice medium-rare. Set the steak aside to rest, and use the same pan to build the sauce. Sweat the shallots until translucent. Add the Dijon mustard and deglaze the pan with the red wine, scraping all the little brown bits off the bottom of the pan. Add the moose stock and reduce the sauce by simmering it for 5-10 minutes. Once the jus is reduced, take it off the heat and swirl in the cold butter to help give the sauce some body and shine.

FOR THE ROASTED GARLIC MASHED POTATOES
1 head garlic
Olive oil
2 lbs russet potatoes, washed and peeled
sea salt and ground white pepper
5 tbsp butter
¾ cup heavy cream

Slice off the very top of the garlic head. Drizzle head with olive oil and wrap in foil. Place on a sheet tray and bake at 375°F until tender and fragrant, roughly 35 minutes. Remove from the oven and let cool. Remove the cloves and mash with a wooden spoon. Place potatoes in a large stockpot and cover with cold water. Add salt and bring to a boil. Cook until fork-tender and drain. Mash the potatoes until smooth. Meanwhile, heat butter and cream until butter melts. Add the roasted garlic and potatoes and mash together. Taste and season with salt and pepper. Serve immediately.

FOR THE ROASTED BEETS
4 beets
Olive oil
Sea salt
Cracked black pepper

Toss the beets with olive oil and season. Bake them in a 375°F oven for 1 hour or until fork-tender. When they come out of the oven, peel away the skins by squeezing the skin away from the flesh with some paper towel. Slice the beets and season with salt and pepper, drizzle with olive oil.

FOR THE WILTED SPINACH
4 cups spinach
1 tbsp olive oil
Sea salt
Cracked black pepper

Toss together in a hot frying pan until the spinach is wilted.

SEAL THE DEAL

86 SPICY SEAL TARTARE À LA CLUB WITH
HICKORY STICKS, PEA TENDRILS AND
HORSERADISH SOUR CREAM

88 SEAL FLIPPER PIE (2.0)
WITH SAVOURY BISCUIT

This is a perfect place in the book for me to go off on a rant about the seal hunt, trying to defend something that I have little personal experience with. However, what I do know is that, if treated the right way, even seal meat can be extremely delicious. When I was a young sous chef working in a local St. John's restaurant, I had the privilege of hosting our kitchen to a Korean chef. He was flown in for the sole purpose of preparing seal dishes in the Korean-style for some of the head honchos involved in the Newfoundland-Korean seal trade. Although I was unclear of the details of their meeting, I had a surreal experience sharing my kitchen with this chef, who spoke little-to-no English. It's funny how food and the international language of cooking can take two people who are literally worlds apart and connect them, creating something so familiar together in such a unfamiliar way. It was an eye- opener to the world of opportunities that ingredients can offer. For me at the time seal was unappealing, as I'd only eaten it in flipper pie. It was grey, over cooked and oily. Together, we took different cuts of the seal and really showcased the versatility of each piece of meat. The seal tenderloin we treated like beef tenderloin, slicing it simply like a beef or tuna tataki, serving it with a fresh wasabi root and soy-like-dressing. The ribs were stewed with vegetables and later grilled like most Korean-style barbequed short-ribs. The flip-

pers were braised and the meat added to a spicy Korean-style kimchi. It was my first introduction to Korean cuisine and most definitely a long-lasting memory that helped mold me as the chef I am today. Whether you support the seal hunt or are dead-set against it, seal a delicious meat. The way they are killed is a dose of reality, but we need to know how our food gets to our plate. In my books, if you know where your food comes from and it's all natural you're ahead of the game. Everyone is entitled to their own opinion, so here are two super tasty seal recipes that will be sure to satisfy even the pickiest of seal virgins.

SPICY SEAL TARTARE À LA CLUB WITH HICKORY STICKS, PEA TENDRILS AND HORSERADISH SOUR CREAM

This recipe is a classic steak tartare recipe with the addition of Sriracha chili sauce and horseradish sour cream. We typically do this recipe at The Club with beef tenderloin, but if you can get your hands on some really fresh seal tenderloin or even horse loin this recipe will take the regular beef tartare to new heights. Homemade hickory sticks add a smokiness and crunch that really put this dish over the top.

Serves: 4

FOR THE TARTARE
1 lb seal tenderloin or beef tenderloin
1 egg yolk
2 tsp Dijon mustard
1 tsp shallot, finely chopped
1 tsp capers
A few drops of Tabasco sauce
1 tsp Worcestershire sauce
2 tbsp olive oil
2 tbsp parsley, chopped
Sea salt
Cracked black pepper
Sriracha chili sauce
1 lemon, zested and juiced
½ cup organic pea tendrils to garnish the dish

Trim the seal meat and chop into small dice. In a mixing bowl, mix the seal meat with all of the other ingredients and season to taste. Serve immediately.

FOR THE HICKORY STICKS
1 russet potato
Sea salt
Smoked paprika
Canola oil for frying

Wash and peel the potato then slice it into long thing strips using a slicing mandolin. Place in a bowl and rinse under cold water to remove any starch. Drain and pat dry on some paper towel and fry in a household deep fryer set at 350°F until golden brown. Season with salt and smoked paprika.

FOR THE HORSERADISH
SOUR CREAM
½ cup sour cream
1 tsp freshly grated horseradish or prepared horseradish
Sea salt
Cracked black pepper
1 tsp lemon juice

Mix all ingredients together in a small bowl and keep in refrigerator until needed.

SEAL FLIPPER PIE (2.0) WITH SAVOURY BISCUIT

This is a really nice variation of a classic seal flipper pie. It combines the elements of traditional seal pie and classic beef stew that you might find in a British pub or French-style bistro.

Serves: 6

FOR THE SEAL STEW
Soak seal flippers in cold water with 1 tbsp baking soda for approximately ½ hour. Baking soda will turn the fat on seal meat white. Using a sharp knife, remove all traces of fat. Rinse under cold water and pat dry with a paper towel.

2 tbsp pork fat back
4 seal flippers
20 pearl onions, peeled
2 garlic cloves, minced
2 tbsp all-purpose flour
1 cup red wine
2 cups beef broth or water

2 carrots, sliced
12 button or cremini mushrooms
2 potatoes, chopped
Sea salt
Cracked black pepper
1 cup frozen green peas

In a heavy-bottomed pan over medium-high heat, sauté both sides of the seal in pork fat, until lightly brown. Season to taste, remove from pan and set aside. Lower to medium heat, add onion, mushrooms and garlic, continue cooking until onion becomes golden brown, approximately 5 minutes. Add flour and continue cooking over high heat until mixture or roux is slightly brown and bubbling, about 4-5 minutes. Stir in the red wine and broth, bring to a boil. Stir until liquid thickens. Season to taste. Return meat to the pot and cover, simmer for 45 minutes or until seal flippers are partially tender. Add carrots and potato, cook for another 15 minutes or until all vegetables are tender. Add the frozen peas and transfer mixture into a deep casserole dish, top with biscuit dough. Bake at 400°F until golden brown. Roughly 20 minutes.

FOR THE SAVOURY BISCUIT

2 cups all-purpose flour
1 tbsp baking powder
1 tsp salt
1 tbsp sugar

⅓ cup butter
1 tsp Mount Scio savoury
1 cup milk

Preheat oven to 400°F. In a large bowl, whisk together the flour, baking powder, salt and sugar. Cut in the butter until the mixture resembles coarse meal. Gradually stir in milk until the dough pulls away from the side of the bowl. Turn out onto a floured surface, and knead 15-20 times. Pat or roll dough out to 1-inch thick. Cut biscuits with a large round cutter or juice glass dipped in flour. Repeat until all dough is used. Place on top of the seal stew in an oven-proof dish and bake until the biscuit is golden brown.

Skate Or Die

91 PAN ROASTED SKATE WITH SMOKED TOMATO YOGURT DRESSING, CAULIFLOWER FRITTERS, TURNIP GREENS AND LOBSTER BUTTER

Skate wing is literally the wing of a stingray fish. It is super tender and is sometimes referred to as the poor man's scallop. Skate is an under-used fish and it can be up there with some of the best fish dishes you have tasted, just be sure to buy it from an environmentally responsible fish market due to their slow reproduction rate. This dish is very simple and you can really use any seafood you want in this recipe.

PAN ROASTED SKATE
WITH SMOKED TOMATO YOGURT DRESSING, CAULIFLOWER FRITTERS, TURNIP GREENS AND LOBSTER BUTTER

Serves: 2

FOR THE SKATE
2 skate wings, skinned and deboned
Flour for dusting
Sea salt
Cracked black pepper
3 tbsp butter
2 sprigs thyme

Season the skate with salt and pepper. Dust evenly with flour and shake off any excess. In a hot pan, sear the fish with the melted butter and fresh thyme on both sides for roughly 2 minutes. Using a spoon, baste the fish by tilting the pan and spooning the hot butter directly over it. Remove the fish from the heat and allow it to rest before plating the dish.
(Recipe continued on page 92)

FOR THE SMOKED TOMATO YOGURT DRESSING
4 large tomatoes
1 cup woodchips, soaked in water
Sea salt
Cracked black pepper
2 leaves fresh basil
1 cup yogurt
2 tbsp sherry vinegar
1 tbsp honey
1 clove garlic, crushed
4 tbsp olive oil
1 tsp smoked paprika

First things first, you need to smoke the tomatoes. This is actually very easy. Put the woodchips in the bottom of a frying pan or wok and put it over a burner on medium heat. Once it starts to smoke take the tomatoes, cut them in half and lay them on a rack that can fit in the frying pan. By this time there should be quite a bit of smoke so you want to cover it tightly with tinfoil to capture all that smoke. Let them go for about 3 minutes and then remove them from the heat. At this point you should be able to just pick the tomato skin right off. In a blender, put the smoked tomatoes along with all the other ingredients and blend into a nice smooth sauce.

FOR THE CAULIFLOWER FRITTERS
½ head cauliflower, cut into florets
1 cup all-purpose flour
3 tbsp baking powder
1 ½ bottles of your favourite beer
Pinch of sea salt
Canola oil for frying

Preheat a household deep fryer to 350°F. In the meantime, in a large mixing bowl, whisk together all of the batter ingredients until smooth. The batter should be thick enough to coat the cauliflower evenly. If too thin, add more flour and if too thick, add more beer. Dip your cauliflower florets into the batter and let any excess drip off. Gently drop into the deep fryer and fry until golden brown.

FOR THE TURNIP GREENS
4 cups fresh turnip greens
1 tbsp olive oil
Sea salt
Cracked black pepper

Toss everything together into a hot frying pan, until the greens become wilted.

FOR THE LOBSTER BUTTER
½ lobster, cooked and roughly chopped
4 tbsp butter
1 lemon, zested and juiced
8 cherry tomatoes, cut in half
5 leaves of basil, thinly sliced
Sea salt
Cracked black pepper

In a saucepan, gently warm through all the ingredients and spoon over the fish while still warm.

NEVER FORGET YOUR ROOTS

Newfoundland is the root cellar capital of the world. We are serious about our veggies and for the most part we have cooking them on lockdown. I mean, any time you put a vegetable in a pot with a chunk of salt beef and boil it, the result is going to be something that you will never forget. Classics are classics for a reason and my nan's Jiggs dinner would be my last meal on earth without any question, but there are so many great ways to cook vegetables. I always say if you can impress someone with a vegetable you know your cooking is legit. Here are a few dead simple recipes using roots to spice up your Sunday roast.

CANDIED PARSNIPS WITH MOLASSES AND BALSAMIC VINEGAR

This recipe turns parsnips from something you avoid with Sunday dinner to the star of the plate.

Serves: 6

10 parsnips, peeled and quartered
¼ cup balsamic vinegar
4 tbsp extra virgin olive oil
4 tbsp fancy molasses
2 sprigs thyme
Salt and cracked black pepper

Place your parsnips on a sheet of tinfoil twice as long as the parsnips and season with all other ingredients. Wrap them up in a little pouch and lay them on a baking tray. Bake in the oven for about 30-40 minutes on 400°F. When done, rip open the pouch to expose the tasty parsnips and serve piping hot.

(See photo, page 95)

FIVE BROTHERS SMOKED CHEDDAR AND TURNIP AU GRATIN

This is a super simple way to take regular turnip mash to new heights. I use Five Brothers smoked cheddar cheese but any high quality cheddar will suffice.

Serves: 6-8

2 turnips
1 pinch of turmeric
1 cup heavy cream
2 eggs
Freshly grated nutmeg

2 tbsp butter
1 cup parmesan cheese, grated
2 cups smoked cheddar cheese, grated
Salt and cracked black pepper

Peel and roughly chop the turnips and place into a large pot. Cover with water, season with salt and add turmeric to help keep the colour bright. Cook for 30 minutes until fork-tender and drain in a colander. With a potato masher, mash all the ingredients together, except the smoked cheddar. Spread the mix out into a casserole dish and top with the grated smoked cheddar. Bake the gratin in a 400°F oven until the cheese is golden brown and serve.

ROASTED ROOTS WITH GRILLED LEMON, SAVOURY DRESSING AND PARMESAN

This is a super versatile side dish where you can literally roast any of your favourite vegetables. The savoury dressing and parmesan cheese creates a golden crust and the grilled lemon adds a fresh flavour that will keep you coming back to this recipe over and over again.

Serves: 8-10

2 potatoes, peeled and cut into wedges
2 sweet potatoes, peeled and cut into wedges
4 carrots, peeled and cut into wedges
1 acorn squash, cut into wedges
1 large red onion, peeled and cut into quarters

12 cloves garlic, peeled
8 tbsp extra virgin olive oil
5 sprigs thyme
Salt and cracked black pepper
2 lemons, cut in half and grilled
2 cups savoury dressing (recipe on page 19)
1 cup parmesan cheese, grated

Cut and place all the vegetables into a large pot. Cover with salted water and bring to a boil for 2 minutes. Drain well in a colander and lay them out flat on a roasting tray lined with parchment paper. Drizzle evenly with olive oil, season with salt, pepper and fresh thyme sprigs. Place the pan in a 400°F oven for 30-40 minutes until all the vegetables are evenly golden brown and delicious. For the last 10 minutes of roasting add the savoury dressing and grated parmesan cheese. Allow it to get golden brown and garnish with the grilled lemon halves.

Sweets and Puddings

I can't think of anything better than finishing a big scoff with a cup of Tetley with Carnation milk and a super delicious homestyle dessert. I love a dessert that brings you back to a place in your childhood. If it reminds you of the comforts of home and still has the whimsy of a restaurant-style dessert, to me, you have a definite winner. These are a few classic desserts that we do at the restaurants. They are super Newfie and super delish, and the best part is, they are not that complicated. Enjoy!

ROASTED PARSNIP CAKE WITH CARAMEL CREAM CHEESE ICING

This is the signature dessert of both of my restaurants. It's been a staple from the beginning and is a really kicked-up version of a classic carrot cake.

Makes: 1 (9-inch cake)

ROASTED PARSNIP CAKE
2 cups roasted parsnips, peeled
1 cup walnuts, toasted
1 cup fine coconut, toasted
4 eggs
1 cup canola oil
½ can of poached pears, plus ¼ cup of liquid
¾ cup brown sugar
2 cups all-purpose flour
1 tbsp baking powder
½ tsp salt
1 tsp cinnamon
½ tsp nutmeg
1 tsp baking soda
1 tsp vanilla extract

CARAMEL SAUCE
1 cup brown sugar, packed
½ cup heavy cream
4 tbsp butter
Pinch of salt
1 tbsp vanilla extract

CARAMEL CREAM CHEESE ICING
¼ cup icing sugar
10 tbsp soft butter
½ cup caramel sauce
8 oz softened cream cheese
½ tsp vanilla extract

FOR THE CAKE

Peel and chop parsnips into small coins. Roast in a tinfoil pouch until golden brown, about 30 minutes. Purée together with the pear and pear liquid. In a frying pan, toast the walnuts and coconut until lightly golden brown. Sift dry ingredients together in a mixer with the paddle attachment. Lightly beat eggs, vanilla and oil with a whisk to emulsify. Mix wet ingredients with dry. Fold in parsnip/pear purée. Fold in coconut and walnuts. Divide into two greased 9-inch cake pans and bake at 375°F for 30 minutes until a toothpick inserted in the middle comes out clean. Allow the cakes to cool in preparation for icing.

FOR THE CARAMEL SAUCE

Cook the sugar in a small saucepan on medium heat until golden brown and lightly caramelized. Whisk in the heavy cream and vanilla. Continue to cook for 2 minutes then whisk in the butter, season with salt and let cool.

FOR THE CARAMEL CREAM CHEESE ICING

In a mixer with the paddle attachment, whip the cream cheese and butter until smooth. Add the cooled caramel sauce, icing sugar and vanilla extract. Continue to whip until the icing is smooth and thoroughly blended. Slice the two cakes to form 4 layers, icing between each layer. Then put the remainder of the icing on top, spreading evenly around the whole cake. Garnish the cake with leftover caramel sauce.

(See photo, page 101)

PURITY LEMON CREAM CRUST CHEESECAKE WITH NEWMAN'S PORT AND BLUEBERRY TOPPING

Makes: 1 (10-inch cake)

LEMON CREAM CRUST
2 ½ cups Purity Lemon Cream cookie crumbs
½ cup melted butter

CHEESECAKE MIXTURE
1 kg cream cheese
4 eggs
1 cup sugar
½ tsp vanilla
1 lemon, zested

BLUEBERRY PORT TOPPING
1 cup Newman's Port
1 cup sugar
3 cups fresh or frozen blueberries
1 tbsp corn starch

FOR THE CRUST
Buzz cookies in food processor until fine. In a mixing bowl, combine crumbs and butter until an even consistency is reached. Pack mixture into bottom of a 10-inch spring-loaded cake pan. Bake at 350°F for 10 minutes until lightly golden brown.

FOR THE CHEESECAKE MIXTURE

In a mixer with a paddle attachment, cream the sugar and cream cheese together until smooth. Add vanilla and eggs, one at a time, mixing briefly. Pour mixture on top of cookie base. Bake at 350°F for 40 minutes until a toothpick inserted in the middle comes out clean. Turn off the oven and let the cheesecake sit in the oven for 1 hour. This will help the cake from forming cracks.

FOR THE BLUEBERRY PORT TOPPING

In a heavy-bottomed saucepan bring the port, blueberries and sugar to a gentle boil. Let simmer for 10 minutes then add slurry of corn starch mixed with a small amount of cold water. Mix well until liquid has thickened. Remove from heat and allow to cool. Slice the cake to desired size and drizzle with the topping and garnish with whipped cream, mint and an extra Lemon Cream.

Every Newfoundlander at some point in time has had a Caramel Log. They're the bomb.com and, as it turns out, they are produced in Scotland. This recipe is basically a deep fried Mars bar on crack. The pairing of the hot caramel with the cold ice cream is unreal. So simple but so delicious.

DEEP FRIED CARAMEL LOG WITH EVAPORATED MILK ICE CREAM

FOR THE ICE CREAM
2 cups evaporated milk
1 cup heavy cream
⅔ cup granulated sugar
2 vanilla beans, split lengthwise and scraped, seeds reserved
6 large egg yolks

Prepare an ice water bath by filling a large bowl halfway with ice and water. Combine the milk, heavy cream, sugar, and vanilla beans and seeds in a medium saucepan and bring to a simmer over medium heat. Stir occasionally until sugar is dissolved, about 12 minutes. Meanwhile, whisk egg yolks in a second large bowl until smooth. Remove cream mixture from heat and slowly pour about 1 cup into the egg yolks, whisking constantly until smooth. Pour milk-egg mixture back into the pan and cook over low heat, stirring constantly until custard coats the spoon, about 2 minutes. Remove custard from heat and strain through a fine-mesh strainer into a third large heat-proof bowl to remove any lumps, scraping as much vanilla bean through the strainer as possible. Remove vanilla bean pods from the strainer and add to the custard. Place ice cream base over the ice bath to cool to room temperature, about 10-15 minutes. Cover and place in the refrigerator to chill completely, at least 3 hours or overnight. Once chilled, remove the vanilla bean pods and freeze in an ice cream maker according to the manufacturer's instructions. The ice cream will keep in the freezer for up to 1 week.

FOR THE BARS
2 Caramel Logs
1 cup all-purpose flour
3 tbsp baking powder
1 ½ bottles of your favourite beer
Pinch of sea salt
Canola oil for frying

Preheat a household deep fryer to 350°F. In the meantime in a large mixing bowl, whisk together all of the batter ingredients until smooth. The batter should be thick enough to coat the bar evenly. If too thin, add more flour and if too thick, add more beer. Dip your Caramel Logs into the batter and let any excess drip off. Gently drop into the deep fryer and fry until golden brown. Drain on paper towel and dust with icing sugar. Serve immediately with the evaporated milk ice cream and caramel sauce.

MARK

Mark McCrowe was born and raised in St.John's, Newfoundland. Growing up around simple New-foundland dishes using fresh seafood and wild game inspired an appreciation for local food and where it comes from. After studying at The Pacific Institute of Culinary Arts in Vancouver, British Columbia and working in some of the city's finest kitchens, Mark re-turned home to further his own individual style as a chef. Opening his first restaurant, Aqua, at the age of twenty-six and his second place, The Club, at the age of twenty-nine, Mark is living his dream cooking food for the people he loves and doing it in a place that means so much to him.

SASHA

Sasha Lawrence Okshevsky was born in Toronto in the '80s. He has worked as a TV camera operator, a host at the World's Expo, a picture framer, an ESL teacher, a visual merchandiser, a bartender, a hand model, a customer service representative, a painter, a window dresser, a visual artist, a dishwasher, a cook, a carnival ride operator, an interpreter, a tattoo designer, a stock clerk, an actor, a photographer, a barista, a graphic designer, a baker, a bicycle me-chanic, a radio DJ and a carpenter, in addition to all the non-paying jobs. He holds a B.A. from Memorial University of Newfoundland and most of a graphic design diploma from Dawson, Montreal, QC. Sasha lives in St. John's, Newfoundland, with his partner Megan Coles and dog Roxanne.

THE RESTAURANTS

AQUA KITCHEN | BAR

AQUA Kitchen & Bar is an eatery located on Water Street in the heart of downtown St. John's. For years it has been an institution for creative casual dining, and has offered its clients great food and service with a down to earth approach that can be enjoyed on an everyday budget. Staying local and sus-tainable is important for our kitchen as it produces the best results for our customers and province.

THE CLUB

Opened in the fall of 2012 at 223 Duckworth in the downtown core of St. John's, The Club is Mark's sec-ond restaurant. Focusing on beer and food pairings, it offers food and drink menus that are a collection of classic and updated twists on pub and steakhouse favourites. The restaurant is casual. The oyster bar specializes in classic recipes like tartare and ceviche using the most amaz-ing seafood and meat. Oysters, mainly east coast, are shipped in fresh and served with mignonettes and lemon. Our draught beer features a line of Quidi Vidi Brewing Company's craft beers, which are a natural pairing with The Club's food and atmosphere.

ACKNOWLEDGEMENTS

Mark and Sasha would like to thank; Mark's mom Gertie, Megan Coles, the Simon/Okshevsky family, Corey Morris, Chad Hussey, Neil Battock, Adam Blanchard, Donnie Dumphy, Lori Butler, all the staff at Aqua and The Club both past and present, everybody in the industry working to make Newfoundland cuisine great and the team at Creative Book Publishing.

We would like to give a special shout-out to woodcut artist Graham Blair, who generously contributed images of his finely handcrafted woodcuts for this project. For information on his available editions and studio visit www.grahamblairwoodcuts.com. Thanks also to Darryl Edwards for letting us use his photographs.

INDEX

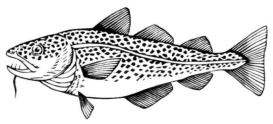

Photo courtesy of Darryl Edwards